To Nancy Big Canoe
April 18th. 1989

Citation of Citizenship

Thank you

Ben Leinbach - recipient
&
Family

1989 - Mayor Gordon Campbell
City of Vancouver

the City

It's hard to write about Vancouver and not say what's been said before.

People who live in Vancouver know the secrets of the city. It offers many unique experiences. Imagine the relief of clear blue cloudless sky after days of grey overcast and drizzle. Imagine English Bay covered with sail boats catching the springtime wind or the spectacle of the mountains after a fresh snowfall. Imagine suffering withdrawal after going two weeks without hearing raindrops on your roof. That's life in Vancouver.

Some get tired of hearing about what a wonderful place Vancouver is from the people who live here. The City of Vancouver presents our city in a special way. It shows the city as it is. I hope The City of Vancouver will help you recall your stay here with warmth and affection. The people who live in Vancouver love the city in spite of its imperfections. After you've spent some time here, I hope you'll be able to see why.

*Art Phillips*

Arthur Phillips
MAYOR

the City

# Vancouver

Broadfoot · Kovach
Herzog · Kenyon
Harvey · Fry · Gilbert

J. J. Douglas Ltd. Vancouver 1976

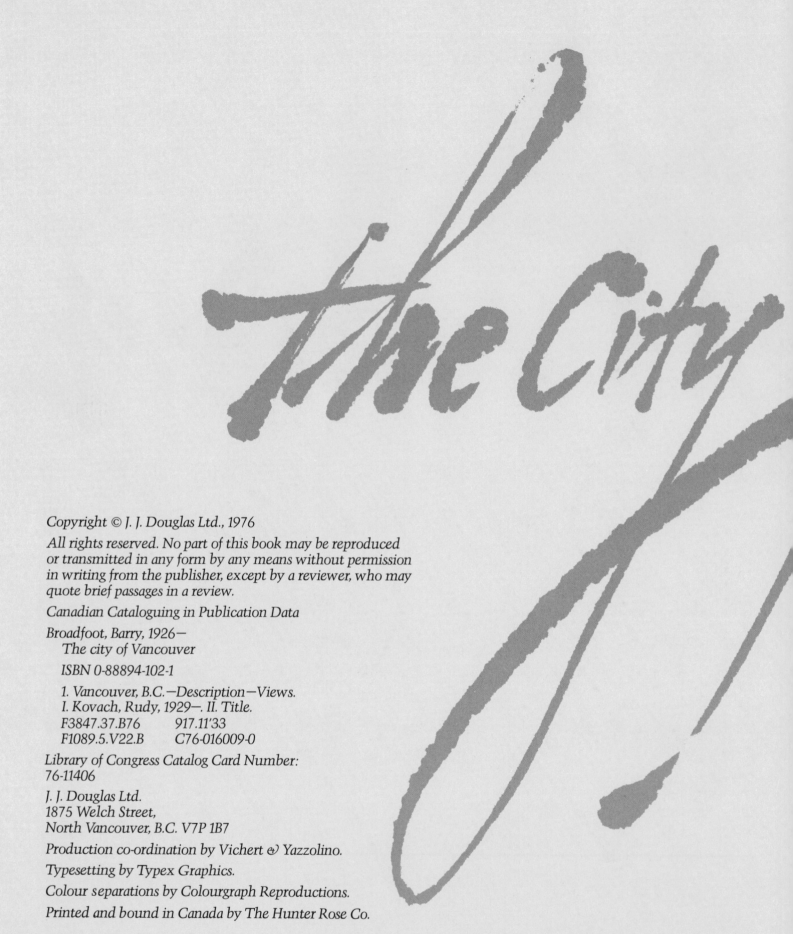

Copyright © J. J. Douglas Ltd., 1976

All rights reserved. No part of this book may be reproduced or transmitted in any form by any means without permission in writing from the publisher, except by a reviewer, who may quote brief passages in a review.

Canadian Cataloguing in Publication Data

Broadfoot, Barry, 1926—
   The city of Vancouver

  ISBN 0-88894-102-1

   1. Vancouver, B.C.—Description—Views.
  I. Kovach, Rudy, 1929—. II. Title.
  F3847.37.B76     917.11'33
  F1089.5.V22.B    C76-016009-0

Library of Congress Catalog Card Number:
76-11406

J. J. Douglas Ltd.
1875 Welch Street,
North Vancouver, B.C. V7P 1B7

Production co-ordination by Vichert & Yazzolino.

Typesetting by Typex Graphics.

Colour separations by Colourgraph Reproductions.

Printed and bound in Canada by The Hunter Rose Co.

CONTENTS:

# I LIVE ON AN ISLAND
*Barry Broadfoot*

*Barry Broadfoot*

# I LIVE ON AN ISLAND,

Bowen Island; six months a year, April through September. In winter I live in Vancouver. My two homes are so close that, as I ride the double-ended ferry *Howe Sound Queen* on her 22-minute chug across the rippled sea to Snug Cove on Bowen Island, I can see to the southeast my city home in West Point Grey. Both homes are embraced by the same sea, sky and mountains.

I call my island "An Island in the City" and my Vancouver home my "City on an Island," and for a West Coaster and a writer, I have the best of all worlds. Here is the ambiance I need—the headlong bustle and zest of the city, libraries for research, the cultural life if I choose it, restaurants of many nationalities, friends; and seven miles away on the island, quiet roads, tall cedars, my small creek, my deer, peace, friends.

This book is about my city on the slopes of the Western sea, as seen through the eyes and lenses of some young Vancouver photographers. I am involved as a kind of relief man. I'll describe the city and its people as I see them, and add a dash of history and anything I believe is relevant, irrelevant, and maybe irreverent.

For I am a True Vancouverite. It was born in me fifty years ago in Winnipeg, although I did not see Vancouver until nearly twenty years later, a soldier boy on leave. Then I knew that this was where I would make my home. The island came later; when the two melded, I had a life plan before me.

Vancouver is not a perfect city, but no city is. You must love Vancouver with heart and soul, while contentedly picking at its many scabs and trying to smooth over its blemishes, or you are just a transient—passing through, metaphorically—although you may have lived in Vancouver for ten or twenty years. To become a True Vancouverite you must lose your perspective; I lost mine in 1944, when at the age of eighteen I spent a weekend leave in Vancouver.

I arrived on a blowy and rainy October night and was billetted with a family in Kitsilano. Next morning, a Saturday, I rode into the downtown area sitting up front beside the bus driver and glancing at the morning paper. As the bus began to reach the crest of Burrard Bridge, I saw English Bay dotted with whitecaps as a strong wind bustled up the inlet; then the long peninsula of Stanley Park in all its splendour of fir and hemlock, coves, beaches, and cliffs; and, suddenly, the protected harbour with the sun polishing the surface, the grey-green slope of Grouse and Seymour Mountains, and the skyline clean-cut as a saw blade. Involuntarily I exclaimed, "Jesus Christ!" People in the front of the bus laughed, for I think they all knew what I was experiencing; although it was a familiar sight to them, in their own way they had the same feeling. Then and there, I left the prairies behind, along with my sense of perspective about Vancouver.

Therefore, what you will read from this point on is one man's opinions about his city. Blame no one else. Some opinions may be outrageous, some noble. A few may be fatuous. I hope the whole is greater than the sum of the parts.

So what is Vancouver all about? People, of course, and attitudes, naturally; but, most of all, the seas around us and the mountains jousting for attention. To the True Vancouverite, nothing else really matters if he has his sea and his mountains. In a 1975 poll, the prestigious *Christian Science Monitor* asked its readers to pick any city outside the United States that they would like to live in. Vancouver was chosen fourth after London, Paris, and Munich. Vancouver undoubtedly was chosen for its sea and mountains, its spirit, its hip and leg and arm action—a lovely girl swinging down Robsonstrasse on her way to work on a bursting April morning. No thought did the *Monitor's* readers give that Vancouver might have grubby streets and mean people, ugly buildings and rotten politics; that it might be barren as the Gobi in things cultural, and without a measure of the sweets of life that make life bearable. I am not saying that is Vancouver. Far from it. Far, far. But when they choose our city, it is for the sea and mountains, because what they see is what they know. The sea and mountains are the inescapable facts of life in Vancouver.

What is this desire to live by water? I don't mean piddly creeks or small rivers. I mean the deep waters of the mariner. Atavistic? More than likely, but through the ages, water has meant transportation and commerce. Vancouver was built on a logging and sawmill economy, fifty cents out of every British Columbia dollar is still based on the forest industry, and this industry needs water—to operate, to move. Many cities are built on water, but however meretricious and alluring they may be, only a few match Vancouver with its gulf, inlet, bays, and river channels, all fashioned in the grand manner, all worthy of epic poems and great novels, and these certainly qualify her for greatness. It hasn't come yet, but it is coming.

Mountains! Let us speak of mountains. Or of the woman from the prairies who was taken to a vantage point by her host, who, with a sweep of his arm, presented her with the North Shore's mountains mantled with autumn's first snows and the high sky above, and waited expectantly. The woman said, "They sort of get in the way of the view, doncha think?" She just didn't understand.

So there is this blending of seas and mountains, blue water and grey rock, and the mix produces something finer in man than man alone can bring up from his soul. There is no way Vancouver could have been built a hundred miles north or twenty miles south. It had to be where it is now. Nowhere is there such an incomparable mixture of heaped-up rock and flecked sea, sand beaches for miles ringing the city, and flatland, shore, basin, cove, and creek as there is in this one small pocket of the world.

We mentioned rain. Does Vancouver have much? Do birds fly? Of course it rains in Vancouver. It rains an awful lot, an average of about fifty-five inches in downtown Vancouver. In a colder clime that would mean about five hundred fifty inches of snow, so to the jibe, "How's your webbed feet?" we say, "We don't have to shovel it." Nobody minds the rain. There are five umbrellas in my two homes and I never use one. I like to walk in the rain and I will do so when I would not walk in the sunshine. I like a soft rain on my face, as soft as the swoosh of an owl's flight through the hemlock forests near my island home. I also like a pounding rain, laving my face. I love to drive in the rain, long distances with a good drink and a good meal in some small, cosy restaurant at the turnaround point. Rain is another inescapable fact in Vancouver life.

When you are elsewhere, in London or Montreal, San Francisco or Regina, and you are asked what Vancouver is like, be sure to have a handful of pretty postcards with you. Even such artless views show why Vancouver is considered one of the ten most beautiful cities in the world—or is it five? And while there are scenes here so miserable, so debilitating to the human spirit, that they make your heart sick, they exist in all great cities. I have seen Rio and San Francisco, Sydney, Hong Kong, and Naples, and I think that all things considered, Vancouver is still ahead of them. We have done fairly well in a century, or even in the last fifty years when the present city's personality began to take shape; or in the past ten years, when downtown business patterns and suburban and residential life styles began to change. Only a few years ago the stumps of once-huge Douglas firs still reared up from many a vacant lot in the city. Now, the vacant lots are gone, and no more are to be had. The city has grown laterally to its full extent and now must grow upward.

And always with us is the realization that we are at the edge of the Western sea.

Some have uncharitably called the journey that brought us here the Westward Tilt. You heave up on the east side of the continent, and all the nuts, the flakies, the adventurers, the sidewinders, the loonies, the seekers and grabbers, roll westward and finally end up sprawled on the shores of the Western sea, spent for the moment but soon to arise and enter the fray. Believers of this theory point to Los Angeles as proof.

The sociologists and psychologists have their own names for the phenomenon, but really it is the old frontier word—"Westering": nations and people on the move until they can go no farther. They have pierced the mountain ranges and now there is the sea. Then they can be happy or melancholy, but they know their trek is over. To move again is to retreat, and for most they have seen the rest and this is the best. They may have found fulfillment of a sort, or believe that they have fled the complexities of the previous life— although of course they will find the same bedevilling situations here. Some come for the climate. Some to join friends. And then there are those who saw our pretty postcards.

Who were they before they came to this city? Or to put it another way, wasn't anybody born here? Well, they came from everywhere; Britishers in the earliest days, then transplanted Easterners, Chinese, Japanese, East Indians, prairie stubblejumpers and disillusioned American professionals looking for a place where they were told the old values still counted. The DPs—Displaced Persons— came after the war, as did the Australians, Filipinos, Germans, Italians, and Dutch. They had seen those pretty postcards or read the letters from friends who had come earlier. The west was settled, by homesteaders who had looked at the pictures; studied the pamphlets; attended the meetings in town halls; read the letters from cousins and uncles about a city on the slopes of the Pacific which seemed fresh and alive, vibrant, on the move, ready to march forward, and with opportunities for all. That's the key word—opportunities. And they found them. They pitched in and they worked harder than most dyed-in-the-wool Vancouverites ever thought of doing, and they built up businesses, established themselves, and in the process some fell passionately in love with the city and lost their perspective to become True Vancouverites.

There are about 1,200,000 Vancouverites. Nobody is exactly sure, because there is a backward-forward movement and how many are on the move at any one time, nobody knows. Actually there probably are no more than half a million living within Vancouver's boundaries, but Vancouver is a city locked in by cities, municipalities, districts, endowment lands, islands—including my island—and it all comes under the aegis of the Greater Vancouver Regional District. So we have conflicts: financial, geographical, social, cultural, philosophical—in a nutshell, who pays for what, or am I getting my share for what I pay? And each resident of each city or district, whether an old pioneer or a newcomer from Brandon, Manitoba, wants his city or district to keep its identity. And so we lump the 700,000 round-abouts in with the 500,000 because, while they may not love our city and actually may distrust us, a great many work in it, live-it-up in it, and sometimes even help to make it all work. Everybody in the regional district has strong links with Vancouver.

My most tangible link—apart from my city home—is the *Howe Sound Queen*. My ferry, remember? Vancouver has always had ferry boats; they are a part of our history. The first ferry, on a triangular route around Burrard Inlet and touching it at the Hastings Mill, was in 1866: so long ago that the world for us was new then.

Since then, there have been ferries to North Vancouver, and through the First Narrows channel to West Vancouver when it was but a summer resort. Ferries now go up Howe Sound, to the Gulf Islands, and to Vancouver Island, and up the coast to Alaska. They're still nice to have around, bustling along like old grannies on an outing. In a city walled off by mountains and cut off by surging seas, ferries provide a means of escape. Or a means to come home. The *Howe Sound Queen* links Bowen Island to the mainland at Horseshoe Bay; ten trips a day in winter, eleven in summer. But in the dark of a February night with a north wind causing her to slip and slide, wobble and roll, going back to my island for a mid-week break, I have been the only car on board, and then I feel she is my very own. She is not sleek and clean of line and she may fit the description of that fictional ship—"She was stubby and square and didn't much care"—but we love her.

My ferry boat allows me to be what I am, a writer living on an island within a great city's regional boundaries. If you ask people in Vancouver if they want to live and work on an island in the city, many would say yes. It would be the romantic and imaginative thing to do; but, alas, they can't. Or wouldn't. There is the inconvenience of going to work every day, across the sea. Where is the drugstore? The butcher shop? The doctor, the baker, the candlestick maker? But what do you want, whipped cream on everything? It is the life for me and qualifies me, living on the outside of the looking glass, to look inside and talk about my city, Vancouver.

On to history. Somebody once said that history is not dull, but that historians can make it so. I'll try not to. So, as they say in story books, once upon a time Captain George Vancouver dropped the anchor of his vessel *Discovery* a few miles south of today's city and set off in a yawl to the north to explore the coast. He sighted the cliffs of Point Grey, turned right, and travelled down the inlet and through the First Narrows into the Inner Harbour where a great expanse of water opened up to his startled eyes. It wasn't the Northwest Passage for which he was searching but it was a great natural harbour, a discovery that most navigators would give their sextants to make. Vancouver wrote: "Here we were met by about fifty Indians in their canoes who conducted themselves with great decorum and civility, presenting us with several fish cooked. These good people, finding we were inclined to make some return for their hospitality, showed much understanding in preferring iron to copper." The date was June 1792. Nothing much else happened. The men of the *Discovery* explored the waters up to present-day Port Moody and some of the young sailors got wet when they went to sleep on the beach and were overtaken by the rising tide. Some sailors!

The Squamish Indians knew the difference between iron and copper because the Spanish had been prowling the northern coast for years, and the Indians had done a lot of visiting and trading. In 1778 the great English navigator, Captain James Cook, had shown up, four years after the Spanish, and a busy trade in sea otter skins developed, with astonishing prices paid in China for the pelts. In 1791, a year before Vancouver discovered the harbour, the Spanish navigator, Jose Narvaez, showed up, marked Point Grey on his chart as an island, and so didn't turn right and failed to find the First Narrows. In fact, as a footnote, he proceeded north and charted my island, Bowen, and named it Isla de Apodaca. Some English bloke changed the name for an officer in the Royal Navy. I would have preferred the Apodaca bit.

When Vancouver discovered the site of what is now Vancouver, it was surrounded by some of the world's finest tall timber. The forest just stood there, untouched commercially, until in 1862 John Morton persuaded two friends, William Hailstone and Samuel Brighouse, to go in with him and buy a lot. They got their lot all right, 550 acres, all of what is now the West End, and for $1.01 an acre. They were going into the coal, brick, and pottery business. Not much came of it and today Morton is remembered in a block-long street near English Bay, and Brighouse for a small district on faraway Lulu Island. And of Hailstone? Nothing. Many of Vancouver's pioneers suffered the same fate. Where are the streets or parks named for restauranteur Brew, storekeeper Webster, lumberman Stamp, hotelier McCrimmon, and so many others?

If we know too little of John Morton, perhaps we know too much about Captain Jack Deighton, a man of much verve who labelled himself Vancouver's first citizen. A saloon keeper!

Another label stuck—Gassy Jack. He talked a lot, in a voice

that shivered timbers, and by talking he usually got what he wanted. Because his was the first saloon on Burrard's Inlet, the little settlement became known as Gastown—unofficially, of course, although it showed as such on British Admiralty charts. But eventually this gave way to the more dignified name of Vancouver. The district, hard by the waterfront, was once the heart of the city, but as the decades slipped by, this area went far downhill and became the home of the rubbydub, the criminal, the loser, and the lost. The loggers stayed in hotels when they came to town to live it up, and the nights were wild and woolly.

Fred Lindsay, an old-time logger, remembered when the old part of the city was still the land of the logger and one of them wishing to go uptown towards Hastings and Granville was kept back by a policeman with a nightstick at the ready. But that was more than fifty years ago. By the mid-1960s, Gastown was a shabby place: old warehouses, greasy-spoon restaurants, cheap hotels, flophouses—Skid Road.

Now, Gastown has become an area of chic and sporty shops, boutiques, and fine restaurants. The rubby and the down-and-outs gaze in wonder as the wealthy, the affluent, the tourists, and the visitors pass by. Crassly commercial, yes, but it is the place to be for the young and not-so-young, and is one of the city's top tourist attractions. And a National Historic Site to boot. The new Gastown really is a fun place, quaint and colourful, and sleek too.

Back to Gassy Jack. Some men have a gift for description, and one of these was Joseph Mannion, an English gentleman. Mannion also later opened a saloon in Gastown, and wrote of Gassy Jack: "He was a man of broad, ready humour, spicy and crisp and overflowing, with grotesque, Falstaffian dimensions with a green, muddy, deep purple complexion that told its own story." So Jack was a heavy drinker.

Mannion continued: "Jack arrived at Burrard Inlet late on a drizzling afternoon, having paddled by water from New Westminster. He was accompanied by his family, consisting of his leman or squaw, her mother, her cousin, a big Indian who was the motive power and on whom Jack cast green-eyed looks, a yellow dog, two chickens, two weak-backed chairs and a barrel of whiskey. Lookers-

16

on remarked it was a doubtful-looking acquisition for the population."

Mannion could have remarked that the settlement, just a clearing pushed back from the high tide line, with its ratter-tatter gang of onlookers, was also a doubtful-looking proposition for anybody intent on the acquisition of great wealth. "Gassy, with the craft of a Machiavelli, began to pass the loving cup with unstinted hand, telling he had come to start a little business, that his means was limited and he would be glad to accept any assistance in the way of building a house. Saws and hammers instantly appeared and the populace, led by a carpenter Mike McNamara, rushed to the work of construction and in twenty-four hours the Deighton House flung its doors open to the public."

That was in September of 1867, four years before British Columbia joined Canada as a province. (Mannion was wrong in calling the saloon Deighton House. Deighton called it the Globe Hotel, and four years later he opened a new hotel called Deighton House.)

In 1869, all there was on the south shore of Burrard's Inlet (now Vancouver) was one sawmill, and a few workers' shacks and a saloon or two (Gastown). When Captain James A. Raymur arrived as the new Hastings Mill manager, he looked about and said, "What is the meaning of this aggregation of filth! I will not permit a running sore to fasten itself upon an industry entrusted to my care." So much for Vancouver. Only a century ago, the area had a population of 146 persons (which then meant white persons of some character), fourteen Chinese, and a collection of ship jumpers, discharged soldiers, Indians, Kanakas, and the drift from the oceans of the world. A most unlikely prospect.

On June 13, 1886, Vancouver was wiped out by fire. Despite the loss of about twenty lives and the destruction of about a thousand buildings, the Great Fire gave Vancouver the chance to start again, after its uneven and haphazard origins. Four days later, a new town was rising. The survivors had plenty of faith, there were speculators on hand to lend them money at high interest rates, and lumber was no problem.

The first mayor and city council met in a small white tent with a board marked "City Hall" attached to it. They sat there amid all the burned-out buildings of their young city and, amazingly, one of their first acts was to again petition the federal government to grant them a ninety-nine year lease on the thousand acres to the west which was to become Stanley Park.

In six months, the city of Vancouver had fourteen office blocks, twenty-three hotels, fifty-one stores, nine saloons, two livery stables, one roller-skating rink, one mill, one wharf and one church, and construction was still going strong. The railroad was coming, and everybody was getting ready. Boom town!

The Canadian Pacific Railway arrived in 1886 in Port Moody. By chicanery, Port Moody was left behind, and the rails were extended up the inlet to the foot of Granville Street. Strangely enough, the CPR just happened to own about 6,000 acres of the adjacent land. That meant they owned the joint. But it was a fact that the west coast was now joined, through the prairies, to the Toronto-Montreal-Ottawa money-and-power-and-politics axis, and the west was saved from an American grab—although not from American domination and exploitation. In those days, the CPR was Vancouver. As late as 1950, the story was still being told of the visitor who asked who ran the town, meaning who was the mayor or chief mover and shaker, and of the city official's reply, "Try the CPR."

Vancouver has more or less grown at the pace described in the Desiderata, all in good time, everything unfolding as it should. The events which did leave their mark on her were external ones such as the Klondike gold rush of 1898, which gave the city a bit of a boom.

When the continent or the world had recessions, depressions—and old-timers will tell you that 1910 was worse than 1935 in Vancouver—then Vancouver tramped stolidly right along. The same with prosperity. What was good for the U.S. was good for Canada and Vancouver, so to speak.

The opening of the Panama Canal in 1914 meant that Vancouver, already the major ocean supplier to the Orient, was also linked to Europe and Britain, as the canal route cut 5,600 miles off the trip to Liverpool. A few years later, Vancouver surpassed Montreal as Canada's top grain exporter.

When World War I began, the city went wild, sending off its

truest and best to the slaughter in Flanders. The pace of development quickened during the Twenties, until the gong sounded in 1929 and just about everything stopped around the world. The Great Depression meant violence for Vancouver, scores of men tin-canning—begging—on the streets, long lines at the missions and soup kitchens, real poverty, and violence as the jobless revolted. It was from Vancouver that the march on Ottawa began, only to crumple like a spent wave in battle in downtown Regina in mid-summer of 1935, and the jobless men were shipped home again.

Then came World War II and more slaughter. Not so much flag-waving as in World War I. In fact, very little. People remembered Spain and Czechoslovakia, and there were grave faces everywhere. The war meant prosperity in shipyards and the airplane factories, rationing, the black market, the hunt for a liquor store with rye whiskey or a hotel with draft beer. A long sigh of relief when it was all over. After World War II, new areas of the city were opened up to housing, and factories turned from swords to ploughshares. What had to be done was usually done—a museum, a planetarium, an aquarium, a stadium, libraries, community centres, public housing, and—the most amusing thing of all—the creation of a town fool for a short-lived reign of capering and poetry reading.

But somehow, through all the years, Vancouver's citizenry felt that if—a hundred years ago, fifty years ago, last year, yesterday—men and women in high places had thought differently, voted more in accord with their consciences, acted more courageously, our city would be a better place in which to live. Vancouver has never fulfilled its political destiny. Where is that great leader—preferably native-born? The city still hopes and waits.

As my ferry trundles across Queen Charlotte Channel, with the towers of the University of British Columbia off to starboard, softened by a misting rain or hardened by splintering sunshine, it takes me to a city which someone once characterized as "a nice place if they ever get it finished." True. It may never be finished. We're living in a new world, one of continuous change. Since earliest days, they have been filling in creeks and gouging out rail cuts, plugging up streets and putting in new ones, opening up parks and then always doing something to them—a road here, a cricket pitch there, a fieldhouse in that corner, and so on. They tore down most of the old town by the water and erected a brick and steel creation.

Now they are ripping up the guts of the downtown and putting up highrises and skyscrapers, and changing streetflow and building tunnels. This phase can loosely be termed: "Let Us All Get Together and Tear Down the Downtown Area and Build it All Over Again." The result has been incredible. Within a few years—almost as quickly as the highrising of the West End—the downtown core from the waterfront west towards Stanley Park and south along Granville and parallel streets has been transformed. Who would have thought so few acres could hold so many buildings? The downtown is ugly yet interesting, and some of its buildings are unique. We have seen soaring orchestration in stone and cement and steel, although some structures have been forever labelled "urinal architecture." There is a mix of many different styles, as diverse as there are new and young architects to design them. Architecture is as much a part of the Vancouver cultural scene as galleries, the theatre, and all the other arts.

Unlike Europe and the East and older North American cities, Vancouver has only one true square, a fact that I find astonishing until you realize, as you must, that the early civic fathers considered business their only business, Mannon their god, and aesthetics a word difficult to define or even to find in a dictionary—but they did win Stanley Park for us.

At the other end of the scale is Chinatown, unchanging in its essential spirit as the decades pass, no matter how many lounges with their fancy decor and neon appear. Chinatown. Also known as Pender Street. Once known as Dupont Street, and then known also for its whores. Vancouver historians tend to shy away from the fact that a waterfront town—loaded with loggers, sailors, labourers, and a generally tough population concentrated in a small area— always has whores. Dupont Street was the street for "fancy houses." Nothing compared with San Francisco's 8,000 whores to 50,000 inhabitants, but they were here in Vancouver too.

Commercial Chinatown now is hardly more than that one street about four blocks long, and it was here that the world-wide revolution in Chinese food began—the Chinese smorgasbord. An abomination, but nothing succeeds like excess. Pender is the street of about twenty restaurants, two daily newspapers, and souvenir shops usually filled with Oriental bric-a-brac but also with fine goods from Hong Kong and China. There is a wok shop, barbers, taxis, tailors (but no tinkers), butcher shops with barbecued ducks hanging in the windows, greengrocers with strange bulbous and tubular vegetables, fish shops with the freshest product in town, and the headquarters of various tongs and fan tan games. Sunday or Saturday afternoons, hundred of the area's 40,000 Chinese roam the street, meeting friends, gossiping, eating huge dinners with at least twelve to a table, and generally enjoying themselves in a mile which is distinctly Vancouver—and ethnic.

Which brings up racism. Vancouver has always had it and perhaps always will, with the pendulum of racial hatred now swinging towards the East Indians from Uganda, who moved with considerable strength into Vancouver's business community. But before that it was the Chinese, the Japanese and the native Indians, and, to some degree, some East European nationalities. During the Depression, there was even prejudice against the English, who, it was thought, were poor workers and unwilling to work ten hours a day for a dollar—but it was just that the English refused to take the abuse that other nationalities had been conditioned to accept. "No Englishmen Need Apply" signs hung on factory doors.

The Chinese have always known racism, from the days of the 1858 gold rush when they came up from the California diggings by the hundreds. Thousands more were brought in to build the CPR and other railroads. Despite head taxes and other harsh regulations, the Chinese kept coming, many legally, many smuggled across the border or lowered over the side of ships in the harbour. They became houseboys, market gardeners, loggers, cooks, honey men, store owners, and fishermen. As the years went by, some became wealthy, some by exploiting their fellow Chinese—but that was business, and Jew did it to Jew, German to German, Scotsman to Scotsman. They survived the exploitation, the anti-Chinese riots, the poor pay, and longer hours than any white man could be expected to survive. When the dawn broke for them, I think they had achieved more in Vancouver than any other ethnic group.

Black people have known hatred, bigotry, and job, rental, and housing discrimination in Vancouver. They still do, but until recent years there were so few black people that one tended to forget they were there.

Not so the native Indians. Since the beginning, they have been terribly abused. When Simon Fraser in July, 1808 achieved his great goal and reached the mouth of the Fraser River, he was hard put to escape with his life when he met the Musqueam Indians at Vancouver, very likely because some early adventurer—a Spaniard, an Englishman, a Yankee trader—had abused the tribe, cheated them, attacked them, or insulted their women. And so it goes, the long litany of sadness involving the coastal Indians—and, in fact, all Indians. Their Arts of the Raven, their magnificent wood carvings were disregarded, laughed at, derided. Their potlatches were abolished. Their legends were held up to scorn, until only the old people knew them. They refused to sing their songs any more, and the old ceremonies almost disappeared. To survive in a white man's world, they tried to be like white men in name, in dress and life style. The white man's diseases decimated them; his rum and whiskey destroyed their morals and their dignity. So, for decades, the Indian might work on the docks, on ranches, in factories, fishing fleets and canneries— but usually when no white man was available. They could be good workers, but few gave them a chance. Now they have a new attitude. They are fighting back and it is the white man, all white men, who are listening and reacting as the native people fight for equal opportunity and compensation for the lands stolen from them. No longer will they accept the white man's domination of their society.

Then there were the Japanese. They had their Little Tokyo hard by the Skid Road, and their village of Steveston and their hundreds of fishing boats, their market gardens, their corner stores, their schools and newspaper. It all added up to the word "ghetto." They would stand up and fight for their rights when other groups wouldn't, but Pearl Harbor did them in. The government decided to ship 23,000 coastal Japanese-Canadian families into the Interior mountains or to the prairies, for each and every one, from grandmother to babe-in-arms, was considered a potential or actual threat to Canada's security. There are prominent men in Vancouver today who gave those orders and carried them out. In this land of freedom, it was an act of unparalleled stupidity and cruelty. Certainly some security measures were necessary; after all, Canada was at war with Japan, and about a thousand fishboats with Japanese skippers worked off the coast. But politics played a part, for it is said that men in high places hated the Japanese, no matter how Canadian they might be. And it was economic, too, for many white men benefitted by the sale of the Japanese boats, lands, houses, and stores, at bargain prices. But they too survived. Now there are Japanese everywhere in Canada, no longer in ghettoes, and the second and third generations are doctors, professors, teachers, store owners, businessmen. And most now smilingly say all is forgiven. But what is forgiven? Man's inhumanity to man?

Racism is the wart on the human spirit, the wen on the gentle face of humanity, and Vancouver cannot look searchingly into the mirror and swear those spots have not been there—or are not there now.

Vancouver has four major residential areas—the East End, the West Side, South Vancouver, and the West End. From the eastern boundary to the west, you can drive and watch the blend, and say, "People on the East Side are poor and those in South Vancouver and the West Side have all the advantages." And you will be wrong. Once, yes, that was essentially a fact, but in a city with a high degree of unionization, high wages—and one of the highest costs-of-living in North America—it cannot be said now. True, many of the houses in the East End are smaller and framed, and their owners work in factories, in lumber mills, on the docks, in light industry and the service industries, but this does not change the beauty of the neighbour-hood gardens and flowers. Block after block, families seem to vie with each other in the care they put into their houses, their flower beds, and their lawns smooth as a golf green. If you drive down the back lanes, you will see expensive power cruisers, campers, seventeen-foot trailers, and swimming pools too. The notion of the poor working class in the East End is a fallacy, and the first to laugh at you will be the East Ender himself. He was very likely born there and grew up there, and that's where he wants to be. He may have the last laugh, for in a town so unionized that it can be paralysed for days and weeks by various strikes, it is he and his union boss, who may be his neighbour, who usually call the shots.

There is a change as you drive from east to west, however, in the larger boulevards, the plantings of trees, the wider sizes of the lots, the newer homes or the older and bigger homes, but there are no more parks or public swimming pools in the south or west of the city than in the east.

Another notion is that in the West End, west of Burrard Street to Stanley Park, there are 50,000 persons living in highrise and apartment-suite misery; or, as one newspaper reporter put it, "a blank stare from every stone balcony, a lonely face from every garden patio." Nonsense. They live there because they want to—high rents and all—so that they can walk to another highrise to work, or stroll down to feed the ducks on Lost Lagoon or play Pitch-and-Putt or just be where the bars, theatres, and trendy shops are. The lonely ones are more likely to be the older people, those who have given up the cares of the family home for the almost antiseptic living of a highrise where they cannot hang their laundry up to dry in the sun and gossip with a neighbour or putter away in their basement workshops.

The West End has been highrised almost out of recognition, but here and there some recluse, some eccentric holds out in an old solid Victorian house with gingerbread trim.

And there are no slums. A waterfront city with no slums? Crazy, but it is true. It is all very well to talk about "The Square Mile of Vice" east of Main Street and south of the harbour, but it is nonsense, a journalist's description. That is merely equating a higher incidence of crime with a lower income level and coming up with a catchy description. There are old houses, yes. Some dilapidated, true. Some that should be bulldozed down. But not slums. A slum has to have slummy minds, where defeat and despair and drugs and alcohol and wife-desertion and crime have taken over, where violence and disrespect for human values are rampant.

How can there be slums where Chinese, many descendants of some of our first citizens, live in peace and tranquillity and industrious labour? How can there be slums where there are many Italians, with red geraniums in their window boxes and bocce courts in their backyards and vino bubbling away in their cellars? And Greeks, with their small restaurants and their propensity to gossip loudly in the streets in little groups. And Yugoslavs, with their ability to make money through hard work and canniness wherever they go. And Jews in their little stores, Norwegians (who are usually called "Swede," just as Danes are), and the English and Scots and French and Japanese and East Indians and Germans—and everyone who is stirred up in this melting pot we call Canada. If you must talk of slums, talk of an individual house in a block, and I will show you slummy houses in every part of the city. Just being poor doesn't make slums. Landlords and politicians also make slums, as you will see in London, Glasgow, Belfast, Paris, Istanbul, Hong Kong, Montreal, and everywhere.

One segment of Vancouver is now gone and few mourn it. In the late 1960s, Vancouver was the turf of the flower people. They arrived by the thousands and made Fourth Avenue and surrounding streets, Gastown, and parts of the West End their Promised Land. They sprawled on the lawns and the sidewalks, the beaches and the benches, and smoked pot and made love and drove some of the staider elements of the city right up the wall. The underground newspaper *Georgia Straight* sold 60,000 copies weekly, and people would say, "Let's drive over to Fourth Avenue and see the hippies."

A girl I knew from Calgary said, "I'm coming out here right after school next year and I'll put on jeans and take off my bra and not wear shoes and I'm not going home until the day before university opens." She didn't come, for the next year the bloom was off. She is now a respectable school teacher. And where are most of the flower children? Some are in communes in the Cariboo and Slocan Valley. Most are respectable school teachers, respectable mechanics, respectable clerks, respectable truck drivers, respectable everything. For that year, as they got more into harder drugs, the petals fell off into the manure, and those that remained became in many ways a dangerous faction, particularly injurious to themselves. How many lives were twisted and torn in that brief three-year era in Vancouver's history? Now, the *Georgia Straight* sells about 11,000 copies weekly. It was a phase a rising and growing city like Vancouver had to go through. It could not have happened in Regina or Edmonton. You see, they do not have sea or mountains, and these things are all part of the mystique, part of everything that happens to this town. Babylon, or Lotus Land?

As this essay has no form, although a fairly resolute beginning, it is permissible for me to break in with random thoughts against the flow. This anecdote illustrates the feeling Vancouverites have for their city and I use it now, for prudence might seize me later. Years ago, when the airlines flew those puddle-jumping DC-3s and the North Stars that destroyed your hearing, there was a tradition that the Vancouverites clapped no matter how routine a landing the pilot had made at Vancouver Airport. Once, after a near ovation, my seat-mate asked what it was all about and I said, "We're clapping because we're so glad to be home." He looked at me with eyes blue and sober as a Scottish magistrate's and he said, "My opinion is that the whole lot of you are just plain daft."

We Vancouverites love our folklore. Another story is that every Vancouverite walks to his garage one autumn morning—we presume he has a clear shot at the mountains—and he must note the first skiff of snow on the Lions. He must remark at the office that there was snow on Grouse Mountain today or, in a bit of one-upsmanship: "Did you see the Lions this morning?"

The Vancouverite must say he loves the boating and that there is no finer sight than Jericho Beach with fifteen or twenty Cal-20s, red and blue and white of sail, running down to the second marker of the Royal Vancouver Yacht Club while their skippers whistle up more wind.

He must say that he goes to the Pacific National Exhibition every year—but only for the agricultural exhibits. Playing Legion bingo, visiting the dreadful girlie show, eating barbecued chicken halves with your hands is out. Out! The barns are the most "in" and it must remind him of his days on the prairies, those eighteen-hour days of toil. Of course, riding the roller coaster is acceptable and so is watching the logger's exhibition of high pole work.

It is quite the thing to go to the Army & Navy's Hastings Street store, downstairs off the lane, and shop for fishing tackle. Cheapest in town and maybe the best.

If you can say, casually, of course: "I saw (naming an important

Vancouver figure) in there buying leaders and we had a chat; he's just back from fishing off Baja California," then fine, that's points for you. But don't be seen buying Levis or underwear. Just tackle.

And each Vancouverite must have a favorite Chinese restaurant, usually some tacky place off Main Street where the waiter knows you so well that he brings out platters of food that the ordinary patron just never sees. It is much better if you can pronounce the dishes by their Cantonese or Mandarin names, preferably in a whining nasal tone, but don't mind if the waiter repeats the dish after you in English.

Vancouverites must not mind the morning and evening traffic, especially on the Lions Gate and Oak Street bridges. If you can say, "I can give myself a pretty good electric shave between the light at Taylor Way and the bridge entrance," that is good. Or, "I can get a pretty good idea of what's in the morning paper between the Airport Inn and Forty-first and Oak when traffic is a bit slow." Do not be upset by Vancouver traffic at rush hours, for it is one of the rites made holy by inaction and time.

And do not be dismayed by civic politics, for it is changeless as the laws of the tide. Remember, whatever party is in power—although they call themselves movements and associations—little will be done except when it is decided by civil servants. Then it will be done. As Nicholas I, Czar of All the Russias once said, "I do not rule Russia. Ten thousand clerks rule Russia." And so with Vancouver.

Vancouver is called Lotus Land, and the lotus—so the Greeks of olden times thought—was a fruit which, if eaten, produced a dreamy and tender forgetfulness which made one never want to return to the land whence he came. Vancouverites are supposed to lie under dogwood trees, chew on a grass blade and watch the cloud patterns form and re-form as they drift. How often has one heard of the executive who, when ordered to return to head office in Toronto or Montreal for a promotion and more money, refused to go? Well, a couple of times anyway.

But is it Lotus Land? Well, we honestly don't know. But we do know that there is no myth about the fleet of cruisers and motorboats sailing through First Narrows from the yacht clubs in the inlet on a Friday afternoon, heading for the sounds and islands off the coast; or the pick-up in traffic as cars loaded down with kids and tents and food and booze head out for the weekend to the Interior, the beaches of the Okanagan, the alpine meadows of Manning Park, or the little cottage, ranch, or farm up some valley. This urge to get away is not exclusively a Vancouver trait, because you'll see it in many cities, but it is definitely a westering trait in the old tradition of the frontier. Not that they can't stand Vancouver a day longer, but there are new things to do and see.

In fact, Vancouver people tend to keep on the move. Firstly, there is a great deal of moving, from district to district, snob mobility all the way. Secondly, there is job movement: upward mobility or the to-hell-with-this-job spirit, and let's try some other type of work. This rootlessness may explain why there does not seem to be that friendliness that one finds—that I have found—in Winnipeg or Regina, Edmonton or Calgary. There is friendliness, but it has to be sought out, even nurtured. Not a real sense of neighbourhood, though.

Vancouver's feelings about Eastern Canada all focus on Toronto—Bay Street, Yonge Street, Bloor and Front streets, Toronto, Toronto! Boo! Boo! Boo! Why, you see you can almost make a passable college yell out of that. And it is all so unreasonable, if you are on Bay Street in Toronto or St. James Street in Montreal or if you are a civil servant looking down from a corner office atop Parliament Hill in Ottawa. But the West does feel hard done by the East, and Vancouver joins in the chorus of resentment. There is this great mistrust about everything Eastern, from freight rates to federalism to *Hockey Night in Canada* (and why don't we see our own team more often?) to the French Question or, as some would put it, the French Problem. There is also an ocean of distrust against the CPR, ranking it after Toronto, Ottawa, and Montreal, in that order.

One Vancouver businessman explained it to me: "I have to get up awful early in the morning to try and beat that Ottawa gang or the Toronto bunch or the CPR. When they're planning something, it sometimes seems to be a smokescreen to hide something else they're planning. Mind you, I said *try* and beat them. That doesn't mean I usually do. The only thing that blows westerly for us is the prevailing wind." One opinion, and shared by many, no matter how unreasonably.

So I sit before a picture window on my island facing an immense western red cedar and watch a squirrel named "Squirrel" sneak away with his peanut snack, and I throw my mind across a few miles of sea to my city and I think of its beauty. I know the Camelot bit with the sun's last rays hitting the West End towers, and I say, "There is nothing to laugh about. It is myth, but it is true."

There are the rose gardens on the dew-wet slopes of Stanley Park, and as you drive to work you only have to turn your head slightly to the left and there they are, and I say, "What a hell of a nice way to start another day's work." I know I am being a bit foolish, but nobody need feel he is a drone, a slave to his machine, a cipher, when he can drive to work and see roses blooming.

I think of a Dim Sum luncheon in a big and booming room in Chinatown on Sunday morning, with a wise old man sitting quietly among his family, a fat, black-eyed baby on his lap.

I remember the bleewww-blaah! of the Point Atkinson lighthouse foghorn coming in my window on December nights, and I recall the story of the newly-arrived prairie man who phoned the lighthousekeeper and said: "Turn off that foghorn. It's been blowing half the night and the fog still hasn't budged an inch."

Downtown, a pretty but weary stripper is taking off everything in a beer parlour before an uninterested gang of juvenile pool players. I trace the undulating movement of the Granville Mall and ask myself if it can succeed, or whether it was just a good idea diffused by compromise. And on the mall, the police, in pairs, stolid of tread, young and tough, move the prostitutes and drug peddlers along.

Dozens of young Japanese businessmen fill up the posher downtown restaurants; I think about how their money has poured into British Columbia in the past decade, and wonder if these men really want to return to Japan, whether the city has got to them too.

I can almost hear the frightening noonday horn atop the B.C. Hydro building, as it blares out the first notes of "O, Canada."

There is Columbia and Hastings, known as "The Corner" across Canada, the centre of the drug trade. A young girl propositions a logger, and the twenty dollars will be used to buy H—horse, smack, heroin. Does she know she signed her own death warrant when she left her upcountry home, a pretty figure, a pretty face, a poor education, and no worldly experience, and entered Skid Road —a down, down streeet in a down, down town for so many?

Ten minutes and a world away are the quiet streets of Kerrisdale, where the upper middle class lives. The children playing in the streets and the Manitoba elms nearly meet in the centre of the road, and a woman wearing white gardening gloves moves among her flowers, so at peace with the world.

A short drive away are the winding streets of Old Shaughnessy, really big houses, all turrets and protruding windows and wraparound verandahs and everything that went with twelve-bedroom houses. If Vancouver had an aristocracy, this is where they lived. I remember a grand old lady discussing the very question; referring to a friend of hers, she said: "And she called herself society, and in this town! Why, my dear, just think of it! Now, if this were Boston..." and her voice trails off.

When I come back from a week in Toronto, I feel like a country boy, and I don't want anybody to feel that way about my town. I think that it is because Vancouver is trying too hard to succeed and is stretching out and up too fast so that the once gracious, if architecturally messy, downtown is now nothing but skyscrapers and parking lots and large holes in the ground. I suppose it shows that the city is on the move, and God knows, it slumbered a long time. The young people who flock here certainly must believe so, for a Toronto magazine has reported that almost half of Canada's creative young people—authors, poets, sculptors, and painters—live in the Greater Vancouver area. It may be an exaggerated percentage, but certainly there are an awful lot of young artists here finding joy in colour or satisfaction in chisel-chipping stone or excitement in stark black-and-white prints coming off a rundown press in a storefront gallery.

Oh, but the unfortunate thing is that if they become famous, then want to become rich they must certainly go to Toronto or New York or London, for that is the way it still is. Take hope, though. The Vancouver Art Gallery had an Emily Carr Room many, many, many years ago when most people thought that Carr was an old lady who painted funny pictures of our rain forests. That room reassures me.

Other things, too, that I love about the city: the ten freighters in English Bay waiting for grain cargo, to Russia, China, the Continent; the window-shopping seamen from all points of the compass, gaggling in a dozen tongues. The realization by local writers, finally, that history is important and that old men should not die with their stories untold. The growing numbers of neat little art galleries in the suburbs. The politeness of librarians and the cheerfulness of under-paid cab drivers, which seems to amaze visitors—the cheefulness, not their scale of pay—and old ladies walking their dogs on quiet streets at dusk. The patience of queues at the bus stops, one of the few vestiges of the British tradition. A long, invigorating walk along Spanish Banks and the man fishing for smelt in his thigh-high green rubber boots. Peeking into his bucket you see only four or five, not much for a morning's catch, when only ten years ago there were tens of thousands for the catching. The increasingly Rabelaisian wit of our morning disc jockeys. Many thanks to the photographer who takes those animal pictures in Stanley Park for the paper.

And Stanley Park itself—the blending of all of Vancouver, sun and sea, sky and water, mountains and brooding Douglas firs, little streams and children at play, and paths for strolling in a world where all the paths are gone. The gabble of the shore ducks off Third Beach moving in and out of a low fog. The old folk retired here who gather by the picnic tables near the Duck Pond and talk away an afternoon, and the people who walk a hundred yards to a litter barrel to keep a beach clean.

But don't forget the mountains and the sea. Don't ever discount them. When you're away from those mountains, you know then, and only then, just how much you do value them. Your eyes seek them and find them not.

Now do you wonder that I still clap mentally, an inward smile warming me, when the 747 brings me here from Toronto or London or San Francisco? For I am home. To my island in the city, to my city on the island.

I could have told you a thousand more things—statistics, figures, percentages—and explained graphs and charts to you, but I haven't. This is how I feel about Vancouver.

# A CITY OF ISLANDS
*An essay of color photography
by Herzog/Keziere/Harvey/Fry
and Wisnicki*

*Garibaldi / Harvey*

*West Coast, Vancouver Island/Harvey*

*Downtown, Vancouver/Harvey*

*Howe Sound/Fry*

*Downtown from Mt. Seymour / Fred Peter*

*Lions Gate/Keziere*

*Coal Harbour / Herzog*

*Royal Vancouver Yacht Club/Keziere*

*Stanley Park / Marion Lucas*

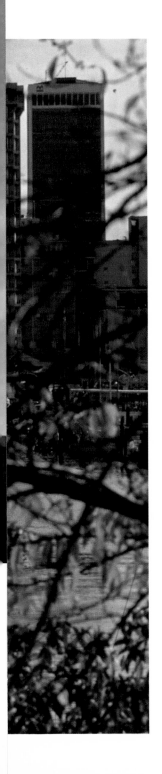

*Vancouver Harbour / Herzog*

CONSOLIDATED
TYPEWRITERS

*Gastown/Herzog*

*Chinatown / Herzog*

*East End / Fry*

Old town / Herzog

*East End / Fry*

*Falsé Creek / Herzog*

*Seymour River/Kovach*

*Steveston/Herzog*

*Steveston / Herzog / Floats / Gilbert*

Steveston/Herzog

Vancouver Island/Wisnicki

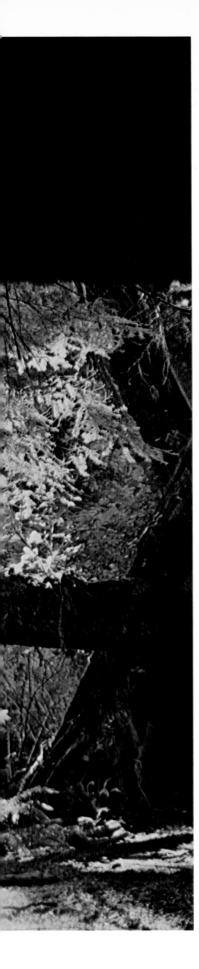

West Coast Vancouver Island / Wisnicki

*Horseshoe Bay / Herzog*

SOUVENIR POST CARD
*Barry Broadfoot*

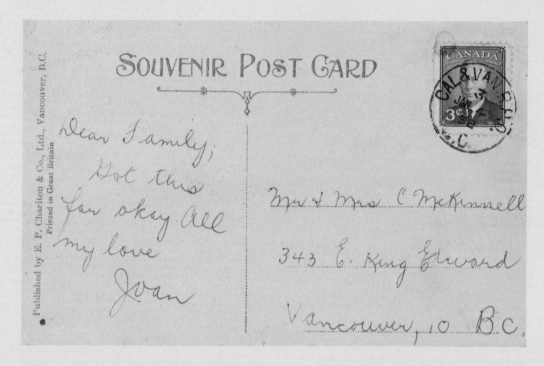

Remember the pretty post cards that inveigled all kinds of people into leaving Glasgow and Turin and Bristol and Topeka to make their homes in Vancouver? They are well worth looking at for they helped make Vancouver what it is today, and they sort of mirror what Vancouverites think of themselves.

I know that some photographers think them vulgar or schmaltzy, but I don't. Maybe too much of a Sunday dress, presenting always the best side, the right profile, but then, that's what they're supposed to do. After all, one doesn't show visitors the back alleys cluttered with overhead wires and cables and strewn with ash cans, so why should the post card?

Gathered together over the years, post cards reveal the history of a city, but unfortunately, they are not like vintage cars or stamps or match box covers; not many people collect them or even keep the ones they receive. A post card is just a throw-away thing because of its trite "Wish you were here."

And yet this small rectangle of cardboard, about four inches by three and a half, is surely one of the best known ways of communicating, putting its unknown inventor right up there with Gutenberg, Morse, Reuters, and Marconi. Strange, our dictionaries and encyclopedias say little of its early beginnings and can't even agree whether to spell it "postcard" or "post card."

If you want to make something out of it, you could go back to about 3000 B.C. when rulers communicated with their captains and each other by having a runner memorize the message, which would be passed on in a relay. Such a message might read: "Capture city. Massacre all survivors. Wish I was there." Later, around 500 B.C., messages were inscribed on clay or bronze and later on wood and bone and these were the first true post cards, for they could be read by anybody who had access to them. It is doubtful if frivolous messages were in vogue and certainly not ones like the one shown: "Dear Family; Got this far okay. All my love. Joan." Where is "this far"? It has a Canadian stamp, so the peregrinations of Joan must have been within the country. Maybe the reverse side showed Niagara Falls.

For all their popularity now—and more than three million are sold in Vancouver every year—the first post cards, called postal cards, showed up hardly more than 100 years ago. Strictly utilitarian. No picture. Just write your message, address it and the job is done. These were sold by the government postal system. Later, free enterprise took a hand and paintings were first used, then black and white photographs; now marvelous bursting colour is virtually the rule. Today the picture *is* the message.

Besides the three million cards sold in Vancouver every year, another million are just tucked into purses to become souvenirs— for a successful post card is one that shares an experience with the visitor. She visits Hadden Park and at the hotel magazine stand that same day she sees a post card of Hadden Park and the 100-foot totem pole and so she writes to her friend in Regina, " I was at this totem pole. It is simply gorgeous," underlining "gorgeous." Twenty years ago that totem pole wasn't there so we didn't have a card of Hadden Park. Now we do.

So that's the way it goes. A post card of logging with oxen in the West End at the turn of the century would be very valuable today, if there were enough collectors around to be able to set prices. But Hadden Park and its totem is history, just as logging near downtown Vancouver is part of our history.

Or shipping. The majestic *Empress of Asia* entering the harbour, her three stacks spiffy as a sergeant's stripes and her passengers thronging the decks to catch their first glimpse of Vancouver. The leisurely Canadian Pacific night boat to Victoria and the day one back—wonderful ships, the *Princess Louise* and her big sisters. Oh, the stories those ships could tell. The stories those who sailed on them could tell. All gone now, all history.

Or downtown Vancouver. You can get post cards now of the bristle of high rises, soaring to create a canyon for the winds below, but I much prefer old Hastings Street, most buildings squat-looking, almost like fortresses, and in perspective giving the street a wider appearance. These cards gave the town a sense of solidity, a feeling of permanence, and they projected a great future.

Rudolph, writing home to his small Bavarian village, selects a post card for his brother with care. Should it be of the natural beauties of Vancouver or that busy street? Bavaria is beautiful, so he opts for Hastings Street, and his brother exclaims, "Vancouver, indeed a great city. Look at those buildings. Solid as Munich," and that might induce him to come to the West Coast. Or again, and these are the chances one takes with post cards, he might say, "Ach, I always thought Vancouver was in the forest. Why, it is just like Munich."

*EMPRESS OF ASIA*

If he had chosen a forest view, Rudolph most certainly would have pondered over the famous one of the hollow tree in Stanley Park. Can there be, over the years, a Vancouver post card more popular than this?

84

*OLD HASTINGS STREET*

HOLLOW TREE
Stanley Park B.C.

Here is proof of the rain forest, the giants of the western slopes with trees so large that when one is hollowed out, a person can drive a car right into it. It could be done sixty years ago and it can still be done today.

Vancouverites speak of The Park. Stanley Park. Canadians might well speak of The Park too, for where is there an urban park to compare? Not Assiniboine in Winnipeg or Beacon Hill in Victoria or Wascana in Regina or Mount Royal in Montreal. Nowhere. Stanley Park is our Chartres Cathedral, our Westminster Abbey, our Blue Mosque, our Hermitage, our 1600 Pennsylvania Avenue. A hundred acres of wilderness, cut by trails through the loneliness and quietness of it all, and two or three hundred acres of pools and

*WHALE POOL  Vancouver Public Aquarium*

picnic grounds; the zoo and the aquarium; playgrounds; places to stroll and watch the Japanese cherry blossoms foam over into a pink blanket or watch the October winds turn the elms into a grandmother's quilt of red, orange and yellow.

It is world famous, as famous as a post card of that pear-shaped stalagmite tip of Manhattan Island, or Big Ben bonging off the hours down through the decades, a symbol of stability as much as the towers of our trees are.

So away we go, best foot forward. Out to Spanish Banks and some walking, watching the ships at anchor in the harbour, a convoy to nowhere. As background, the mountains of the North Shore against a sky as blue as a robin's egg. Well, sometimes. Sometimes, and in fact quite often, that sky can be grey as a gull's wing.

*TOTEMS in Stanley Park*

The Nitobe Gardens. Japanese Canadians take their Japanese visitors there. You see them often. Do they wonder how we have managed to do it so well, or are they just homesick? Perfect in its symmetry, lovely in its summer dress. No tea ceremony, though.

*NITOBE GARDENS  University of British Columbia*

To the North Shore and out the winding Marine Drive, complete with its Suicide Bend, to Whytecliffe Park and the lighthouse. An honest-to-God lighthouse, on a rock, going "burp" in the night.

*LIGHTHOUSE PARK  West Vancouver, B.C.*

And out the Seaview Highway from Horseshoe Bay. Not far, mind you. A couple of miles will do, but there are places for a perfect view of Howe Sound, our Inland Sea, with its grey green mountains and

*HORSHOE BAY  West Vancouver, B.C.*

old Mount Tantalus and his snow fields rearing up miles away to the north. I love that old mountain. If mountains could smile at visitors, he would.

*AERIAL TRAMWAY Grouse Mountain*

*BAYSHORE INN Vancouver, B.C.*

Try the skyride to Grouse Mountain, but only if it is clear. Preferably at night. There below, the city. Take it, it's yours. The giant grids, the strings of lights extending away to the far shore, freighters entering harbour, the velvety feeling of it all, and around you young, fresh-faced, red-cheeked hikers or skiers coming in from the hills around. No wonder they call Vancouver a young city, a sports city, an open city. The mountains draw the young and energetic.

Down to the planetarium. Watch the giant, soundless machinery of night move the stars through their paces. The museum. Take your time. Nobody learned anything walking quickly through a museum. Ask where the *St. Roch* is berthed, sitting rather self-consciously in her nice bed of concrete under her tent-like roof after all those years of braving the pack ice of the Arctic.

*CENTENNIAL MUSEUM and PLANETARIUM*

Simon Fraser University. From a distance sitting like a medieval battlement awaiting the invader. Walk through its concrete corridors, watch the faces, Anglo-Saxon, East Indian, Slavic, Scandinavian, Chinese, Japanese, Indian, French, and you realize that here is a university with a special joyousness to it, a university born of an instant mix of architectural genius, bulldozer, concrete and desks. And it worked.

And another kind of building, Totem Park at the University of British Columbia, an open-air building, the walls unevenly spaced totems of long ago and the roof the open sky. But here, as at Stonehenge, one feels the need to bare one's head as if entering a cathedral, for it is almost a holy place, a memorial to great men, the carvers, the protectors of the mythology of the coastal dwellers.

90

MARITIME MUSEUM *Hadden Park*

*SIMON FRASER UNIVERSITY*

Vancouver relaxes. Mañana country. Lotus land. True and not true, but nowhere more than at fair week at the Pacific National Exhibition, going strong each summer since 1910. Where you can watch the loggers at their dangerous play, smell good pungent cow manure in the barns and soar back over the decades to your life on

91

the farm, play the games and win a giant panda, watch the ponies run. Oh such a variety of things to do. It is as if giant hands had taken all the pleasures of the summer's day and poured them into a funnel and they spilled out here. I once saw two boys, no more than ten years old, eating plates of chow mein and sweet and sour spareribs

LOG ROLLING  *Pacific National Exhibition*

FERRIS WHEEL  *Pacific National Exhibition*

at a Chinese booth not five minutes after the fair had opened at 10 a.m. one lovely morning. That's really taking one's pleasure as it comes.

And so you can go on and on; take the miniature train through Stanley Park and watch the Arctic wolves endlessly pacing in their cages or ride the Royal Hudson, a huge and shiny steam engine, up to Squamish for a day. You can watch cricket at Brockton Oval, all very proper, and then stroll over to the pool and watch another species, the penguins, as proper in their black suits and white vests as Parisian waiters in the Rotonde cafe.

*MINIATURE TRAIN  Stanley Park*

So as we said, a considerable part of the message sent back to Binscarth, Manitoba, to the folks, or the card sent to Aunt Jane at Cheam, Sussex, England, has really little to do with what it is all about. What it is all about is on the other side, the pretty picture side. The message itself can be puerile, banal, ridiculous, non-informative, a waste of time, but the picture is the thing. "I was there," and even if it is a post card of your hotel that you found in the stationery drawer, an "X" on the window of your room means something.

And we, the people of Vancouver, become perambulating post cards ourselves in a strange way. When the folks from Binscarth, Manitoba, or Aunt Jane come to town, we take them visiting. And

*HOTEL VANCOUVER*

*LITTLE MOUNTAIN CONSERVATORY*

where do we take them? To all the places, to all the pretty pictures on the post cards, for we recognize that these places are the best, the most beautiful, the most truthful.

94

*ROYAL HUDSON Vancouver to Squamish*

When the long tour is done, there is a very good chance that the last stop will be on the shore, by the sea, looking across the bay.

When our visitors leave, we return to our ordinary ways and to our private views of the city: the ones we see on our way to work and to the shopping centre and from our garden. But we know that the beautiful post card views are there when we want them.

SPECIAL WORLDS
*Studies by Robert Keziere and*
*Herbert Gilbert*

*Gilbert*

*Keziere*

Herzog

Reflections / Gilbert

Skyline/Gilbert

*Burrard Drydock / Gilbert*

*Burrard Drydock / Keziere*

122

Burrard Drydock/Keziere

*Burrard Drydock/Keziere*

*Burrard Drydock/Keziere*

Burrard Drydock/Keziere

*Rain / Keziere*

*Rain / Keziere*

Stock Exchange / Keziere

Stock Exchange/Keziere

*Stock Exchange/Keziere*

*Newsboy/Keziere*

Downtown/Gilbert

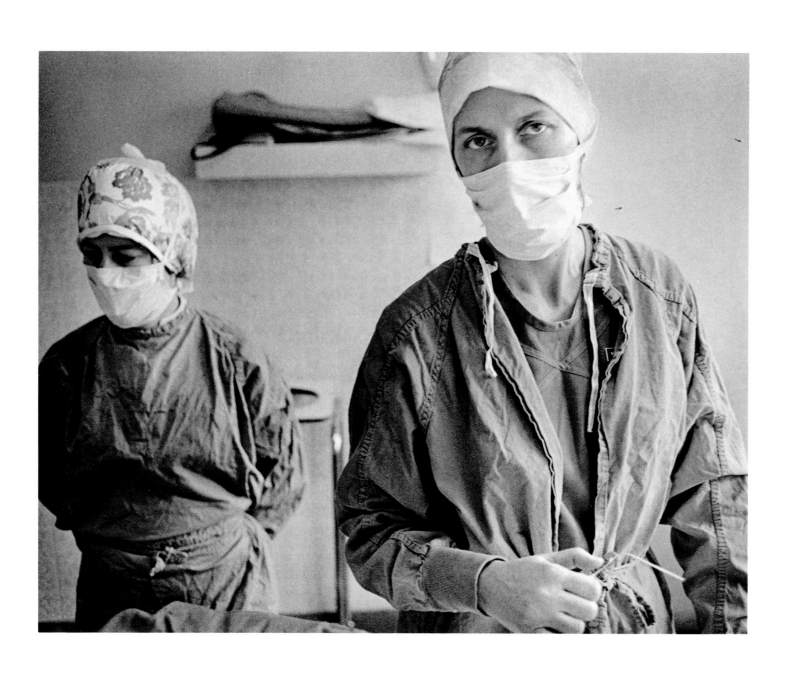

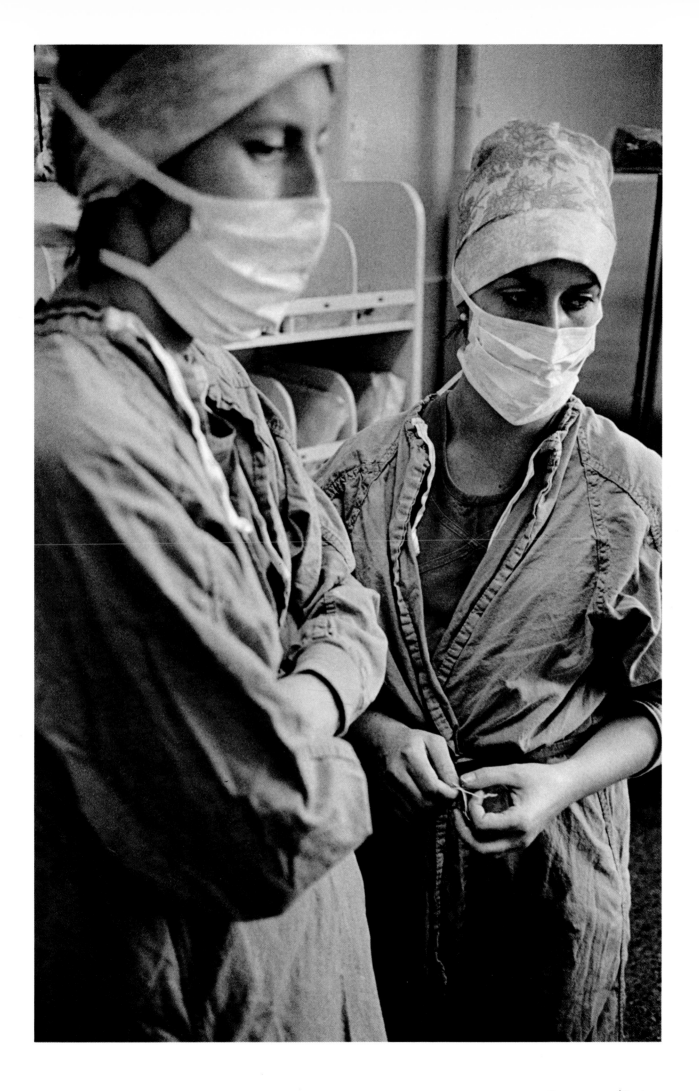

*Downtown/Keziere*

148

*Downtown/Gilbert*

*Downtown/Gilbert*

# DOWNTOWN
*Principally by Fred Herzog*
*Some views of the City as a place to*
*live—and as a lived-in place*

*Cathedral/Gilbert*

*Old town/Herzog*

*Old town / Herzog*

*Windows/Herzog*

*Old town / Herzog*

Old town / Herzog

*"Skana"/Stephen Miller*

Rugby/Fry

*Watchers/Herzog*

*Greenpeace Whale / Thomas*

English Bay / Herzog

*Finish Line, Bathtub Race / Herzog*

*Kites in Vanier Park/Fry*

*Herzog*